Finding Jesus in the Mess

By

Christine Slattery

Christine Slattery

Published by AJ Creative Writing Coach & Editor LLC

"Finding Jesus in the Mess"

Library of Congress Cataloging in Publication Data AJ Creative Writing Coach & Editor LLC

ISBN: 978-1-7360684-9-6
Library of Congress Control Number: 2022912051

Author: Christine Slattery
Editor: April Johnson

Publisher & Editor
AJ Creative Writing Coach & Editor LLC
Website: ajcreativewrites.com
Email: info@ajcreativewrites.com
Phone: (877)647-0179
Saint Louis, MO

Table of Contents

TRIBUTE

This honor and tribute are to my mother, whose intimate relationship with Jesus piqued my curiosity and inspired me to seek to know Jesus personally. In addition, to my family, you know my heart's deepest desire. I love you all.

Prologue

We prefer the smooth sailing, quiet breeze of the still sunlit sea, but sometimes God leads us up mountains, into valleys, and the terrain where we would rather not explore. For years, a persistent prompt presented itself during prayer to share my life's reflections that resonated with His voice through prayer and scripture.

I spent quiet time with the Lord in the chapel one early December day. I felt the nudge again. I candidly responded to the nudge, "God, if you want me to write a book, you better give me the title!" Forgetting my prayer, I proceeded home to pull out the Christmas decorations. Our beautiful nativity set, adorning my piano, was a gift from my mom and sister. As a custom, the remaining figurines from the old nativity set, which happen to be the Holy Family, take a principal place in our kitchen as a reminder to keep Advent focused on Jesus. I rummaged through a box and found Mary and Joseph, but I could not find baby Jesus. I thought, “Look at me trying to find Jesus in the mess!” My next immediate thought was, “Sounds like the name of a book!” At that very second, I recalled my conversation with God just an hour earlier in the chapel: “God, if you want me to write a book, you better give me the title!” God responded to my flippant, candid prayer and gave me the title that befits my written material. I did not want to heed God’s call to write this book. Just as Moses in the Bible did not want to heed God’s call to lead the Israelites out of Egypt, he felt inadequate for leadership.

This book is certainly not a theological masterpiece; instead, it is a series of reflections based on one simple woman’s search for God in the joys and tribulations of life. It illustrates movements of God’s grace, woven through the incidents of life to awaken my attitudes and awareness of God’s presence as He called me into greater intimacy with Him through life circumstances.

God exposes fears, reveals truths, teaches, forgives, and heals. He draws us closer into His presence as we establish a devoted relationship with Him. My prayer is that this book may help other people experience a vibrant, loving, intimate relationship with Jesus.

My greatest desire in life is for everyone to have a personal relationship with Jesus and experience His love, joy, strength, and peace throughout life's journey. However, I do not have the power to orchestrate that relationship, but I can share firsthand experiences that led me into a more personal relationship with God. Prayerfully, my experience will radiate and draw others to Christ. They will have an opportunity to open their hearts and learn the difference between knowing *about* God versus intimately *knowing* Him through experience. How we live now and align ourselves with Christ directly affects our eternity. Our life on earth is minuscule with eternity as the backdrop. It is an unpopular message, but it is the truth! Be vigilant! Be wise! Do not put off welcoming Christ into your life.

Even though heaven is our ultimate goal, those who accept Christ into their lives on earth become more spiritually aware and can talk to God more freely. They can also see God's grace, mercy, and hand in their healing on all levels—spiritual, emotional, mental, and physical. The Holy Spirit sharpens our senses to hear God's voice, discern His ways, and follow His plan for our lives. Another benefit of having a genuine relationship with God is that joy and peace overflow into our lives amid the turmoil. God's peace will be a testament to His glory.

God made us for His goodness and glory. We were created to become ambassadors for His kingdom. He desires for us to be His face in the world, displaying His honor and glory. God is communal and desires relationships with everyone. Imagine if we all consciously loved unconditionally like Jesus and let God's light shine in us and through us! Can you envision how much more peaceful the world would be if each person surrendered to God's will for their life? Not just to live a "good" life, which is arbitrarily defined.

When we grow and mature spiritually in the knowledge of Jesus Christ, the incarnate Christ becomes more apparent. When blinders are lifted, it is easier to see His embodied love. He cares! He listens! He forgives, heals, blesses, and guides us! He works through humanity to serve as His hands and feet in this life. He accepts our current state and loves us enough to invite us into a more passionate union with Him, so that we can reflect His image. God accompanies us through each moment of life. We have no control over life's highs and lows; whether we are aware of it or not, He is with us along the way. Often, God uses life's low points for us to find "Jesus in the Mess" of Life. Spending time with God makes us more sensitive to His presence next to us and within us. All too often, we set our daily agendas without consulting God. We can consult God as He reveals Himself in His divine persons.

I will interchangeably reference the three persons of the Trinity: God our Father, Jesus Christ, and the Holy Spirit. I acknowledge their oneness but identify each person according to my personal experience. One night, as I nestled into bed, I asked God to please give me the format for my book. I awoke in the middle of the night, verbally repeating, "Short chapters, reflection questions." As I gained awareness, I wondered why I repeated this phrase and immediately recalled the prayer petition as I rested my head on the pillow, "Please give me the format for my book." The format of this book consists of short passages followed by reflection questions to stimulate contemplation and discussion. It may be practical for those who enjoy journaling to journal their responses.

"For my thoughts are not your thoughts, nor are your ways my ways, says the Lord. As high as the heavens are above the earth, so high are my ways above your ways and my thoughts above your thoughts." (Isaiah 55:8-9)

ARE MY WAYS GOD'S WAYS OR THE WORLD'S?

Years ago, I recognized the need to pray for world peace. I knelt, absorbed in prayer, asking God to bring peace into the world, the inner-city war zones, and to domestic violence victims in homes. Surprisingly, Jesus and our Blessed Mother Mary revealed themselves to me through magnificent love that permeated with abundant peace and the sweet aroma of roses. It was as though heaven descended just to touch my heart.

The prayer service ended, and my new life in Christ began. I knew my life had changed! I prayed for peace "out in the world," but God's plans for my life prevailed.

Transformation miraculously occurred in my life; through Our Blessed Mother, the Holy Spirit invited me on a journey into insightful awareness and a relationship with God. I received a divine peace and a desire to know God and discover my faith as an adult. God was preparing me for the journey forward.

The next day, I saw life through new lenses and perceived the invitation to know, love, and serve God with a new spirit. I consciously decided to make Christ the center of my life. My transformation started when I was a young mother, frustrated with the lack of perfection around me. I instantly lost it over "spilled milk" or felt resentment, bitterness, and anger when things were not done my way. I was currently serving abundantly, but God wanted to show me a better way – His way. As I allowed God to lead, I united with Christ, *"As I have loved you, so you must love one another," (John 13:34).* Even though I loved marriage and motherhood, my efforts lacked love and compassion. God's voice of wisdom spoke to let me know my ways deviated from His ways and that He had tremendous grooming to do in me. He will forever shape me in His grace through life experiences and relationships. I was inundated with volunteer obligations before God stepped in and strategically prioritized my family life. Sometimes I spent every night of the week at meetings. At the same time, my husband remained home with our four young children. I was hardly working within the context of my vocation. I recall reading a book, "The Apostolate of Holy Motherhood," which emphasized the importance of my primary vocation as a wife and mother. I liked being a mom, but I realized I was too busy and didn't appreciate God's gifts. I was too preoccupied and busy, wrapped up in worldly ways and going in the wrong direction. As I readjusted priorities, God dropped resources and spiritual friendships in my path that redirected my trajectory. A more dedicated prayer life resulted in changed behavior and more loving attitudes on my part.

I had a greater yearning to attend prayer groups, scripture studies, and studies on church teachings. God prepared me for the challenges ahead. His love equipped and taught me to live according to His will. *"God is love," (1 John 4:8).* He teaches us agape love, pure love. Surrendering our hearts to Jesus allows our egos to decrease and the spirit of God to increase in us. In doing so, He gives us spiritual insight and equips us for foreseen and unforeseen circumstances. God wants us to align with His will and live in freedom.

At times, we function as though we will lose our freedom if we follow God; that is too much, too difficult, constraining, or boring. Knowledge arms us with the truth; allows us an opportunity to gain freedom from deceit, internal lies, self-centeredness, hurts, wounds, and self-pity that keep us stuck from accomplishing God's will for our lives. After studying scripture for some time, it became evident that *"the truth will set you free," (John 8:32).* Life is happier since I have *"approached the throne of grace," (Hebrews 4:16).* The biggest surprise is that living in the truth is more gratifying than living in denial or ignorance of scripture and church teachings.

REFLECTION

1) Am I willing to learn more about God and let Him draw me into a deeper relationship with Him? Have I studied my faith as an adult?

2) We all have moments of resistance. What stands in the way of my approaching God and establishing intimacy with Him? (i.e., time, business, fears, feelings of betrayal, apathy, unworthiness, etc.).

3) God calls through ordinary interactions. In light of current events, how is God calling me to align my life with Him? Do I believe He will respond if I open myself to Him? Do I trust His plan for my life? Will it bring happiness?

4) What commitment can I make today to advance my spiritual life with God?

"Know that the Lord is God, our maker to whom we belong, whose people we are, God's well-tended flock." (Psalm 100:3)

IS YOUR RELATIONSHIP WITH GOD PERSONAL OR IMPERSONAL?

Personal relationships entail spending time together, often communicating, and learning one another's likes and dislikes—equally the same when spending time with God. One means of spending time with God is communicating with Him in prayer. Prayer is a two-way communication between an individual and God. God listens to our prayers as well as speaks to us in prayer. He communicates with us through others, creation, the Bible, and life events. God gives us scriptures to comfort and guide us; He uses people as His human mouthpiece, a human vehicle to deliver His message to His people. He also speaks to us through dreams and various states of affairs. God knows each of us so well that He numbered the hairs on our heads. He wants us to have the same passion when getting to know Him. God wants to know who you say that He is.

"Jesus Christ is the image of the invisible God," (Colossians 1:15). Who is Jesus to you? Be careful to distinguish personal opinions and impersonal knowledge from the truth. Based on life experiences, we can acquire false impressions or opinions about Jesus. To know the truth about who Jesus is requires communing with Him, reading His life stories, and meditating on His humanity and life responses. While teaching through example, Jesus always focused on the Father and responded with love and compassion to everyone. He healed the sick, blind, and lame, and cast out demons. He called the weak to leadership and humbled the proud and arrogant. He received the children, the poor, neglected, shamed, and wayward. Jesus exemplified in life and through death an unwavering unity with the Father. This is the real Jesus! The reality of who Jesus is becomes distorted

through humanity's brokenness. Our feelings and challenges parallel Jesus', but He is our divine resource. Jesus not only set standards but lived by them. He is the perfect model to follow in the search for spiritual growth. He always teaches us to love deeper and savor His friendship no matter the circumstances.

In my earlier years, my image of God was of a stern, gray-bearded old father figure with his hand outstretched, pointing His finger to correct me. He was a critical, unapproachable, unaffectionate, cold figure. My image of God has changed through the years as I prayerfully healed through certain pain I encountered. It takes time, commitment, and discipline to face painful memories and fears from the past, but when confronting the past with God, He endows us with His Spirit and reveals the truth of His love. We have a perfectly loving Heavenly Father.

I loved my dad, but he was critical, authoritarian, controlling, and stifling, which bred a sense of unworthiness, insecurities, a lack of confidence, and a loss of voice. I lacked the confidence to make my voice heard and learned only to express what I knew would be accepted without criticism. I learned not to trust my ideas. I sensed a need to be perfect (unrealistic expectations). I mustered up enough courage to acknowledge that it took a toll on my life and how it affected my family's life. I petitioned God in prayer and eventually collaborated with a spiritual director who uncovered the lies rooted in the false identity instilled in me during my childhood by my parents' parenting style. Recognition alone was grace, coupled with God's grace to see the truth about myself. The spiritual director's expertise brought fresh insights to light, allowing me to love myself and my parents through their imperfections. I, too, am an imperfect parent. My parents were well-intended yet broken in their own way, and God helped me understand, forgive, and adopt new, healthier thought processes and behavioral patterns. Now, with a healthier perspective, my image of God is gentle, loving, consoling, and warm. He embraces me with hugs. He attends to anyone I place in His care and ministers to our needs. He desires greatness, loves beyond comprehension, and receives everyone, no matter how broken we are. He is not critical but open, compassionate, non-judgmental, and patient. He is the Power that restores broken relationships in my life and helps me cope with conflicts. He is my friend, whom I run to in times of need and thanksgiving. Praise flows forth to honor Him in His greatness. He is my constant companion, consistent and always ready to forgive. Through prayer, God has revealed His true nature.

REFLECTION

1) Meditate on who Jesus is to you.

2) Is your relationship with Jesus personal or impersonal? Studied or an understudied impression?

3) Do you believe that God invites you to open the gift of His love no matter where you are in your faith journey today? Do you want to know His love more fully?

4) Commit to fostering a deeper love relationship with God. Be realistic, and each day, recommit your desire to God to draw closer.

"We appeal to you not to receive the grace of God in vain." (2 Corinthians 6:1)

"Grace is favor, the free and undeserved help that God gives to respond to his call to become children of God..." (1996) It is a "participation in the life of God" (1997)." The Catechism of the Catholic Church.

WHAT IS GRACE? RECOGNIZE MOVEMENTS OF GRACE IN YOUR LIFE

God generously offers grace. He is the giver of all grace that multiplies blessings. Grace is God's supernatural power that expresses His love in us, to us, and through us. God's grace works in various capacities in our lives. His grace enables, favors, and equips us in trouble. God provides sufficient grace to encounter every problematic situation. God extends grace in both big and small problems. Life will present discouraging situations, but by God's grace, you do not have to be discouraged, bitter, angry, or feel inadequate. You can surrender every negative emotion to the God of all grace. Grace speaks in desolate (lonely) conditions that amplify weakness. God's grace allows us to exchange our weakness for His strength. The Lord promises saying, *"My grace is sufficient for you, for His power is made perfect in weakness," (2 Corinthians 12:9).* We need God's grace to receive God's divine help and strength in times of need. God uses our problems to grow in grace and mature us spiritually. Spiritual growth empowers us to grow in the knowledge of Christ to propagate charitable deeds that beget wisdom, knowledge, joy, inspiration, and understanding for a dying world that God so loves. It is total favor from God, who generously imparts unmerited blessings to all. He loves and longingly invites everyone into his inheritance. Through faith, grace conforms souls to Christ to escape eternal damnation.

Grace inspires individuals to pray with expectant faith and believe God cares enough to answer. Grace develops belief and trust that God will deliver an answer to our prayers in His perfect way. When you do not know what to pray, call out Jesus' name. He knows your desire and understands that you seek grace in desperation. Call upon Him! Ask Him for the miraculous with expectant faith that moves mountains and heals the unforeseeable. Rest in knowing that God's grace alone will alter a course of action and bring transformation that goes beyond limits. His grace heals physical, emotional, and spiritual pain beyond medical experts' understanding. It is not "I" who turns to God, but God's grace turns me to Him. The Holy Spirit prompts us with His grace to seek God, pray, believe, and trust Him. God's grace is the merciful gift that transforms docile souls.

It would be short-sighted to speak about grace without mentioning God's mercy. In the Old Testament, sacrificial offerings were made to regain favor with God. In the New Testament, God gives us his Son, Jesus, in the flesh, the final sacrificial Lamb, who died for our sins to be wiped away. Jesus's sacrificial Blood washes over us to free us from the burden of sin! Jesus demands nothing from us except an openness to receive His grace and mercy. All He wants to do is to bestow His mercy on us. He does not require perfection. He accepts us as we are, sin and all, so that He can embrace us and pour out His mercy His life-changing grace — on us. The invitation has already been extended to receive Him into our hearts. All God wants is for us to surrender to His invitation! Be an open vessel to receive His merciful love.

God's grace extends free will. We have the choice to cooperate with God's grace or refuse it. Faith and grace intertwine to supply our spiritual needs. We must cooperate with an act of faith for transformation to occur. Grace has power over sin to loosen the hold of sin and give strength to the sinner to break free, but the sinner must believe, accept the grace, and act in faith for transformation to occur. Catholics have the privilege of receiving healing grace through sacramental reconciliation. Bring all your shortcomings and sins to the Lord and admit out loud that you have a problem. Then, renounce it; "I no longer want to carry _________, the weight of sin!" If tempted to recommit the sin after surrendering it to the Lord, refer to the sacramental grace received and use it; choose faith and use the grace bestowed through the sacrament so that the sin may have no power over you. Believe in the power of sacramental grace, which is a gift liberally granted by God for personal sanctification.

Christ died for our sins. Consequently, our sins are forgiven, but there is a prerequisite. Imagine yourself standing before Christ, holding onto anger and unforgiveness towards another; Jesus says, "Give it to me. Give me your anger and unforgiveness. I died so that you would be free from the bondage of all sins; therefore, release them to me so that you may be free. You can only be free if you allow me to take them and pour my mercy over them." This demands a conscious choice to release them or hold on to them. To cooperate or not with the grace that has already been bestowed. Whatever happens, Christ has already died for sins and loves the sinner, but it is a personal choice whether to hold on to sin or surrender and accept the grace that renews your spirit. When we release the pain to Jesus, He can fill the once pain-filled space with His light, peace, and joy to set us free from the bondage of sin. We may still carry a negative feeling about a deep-rooted hurt, but we can respond with genuine Christian forgiveness and a loving attitude through God's grace.

GRACE IS A PROVISION

How often are random coincidences in life really "coincidences" and not God's graceful plan revealing itself? I reflect on the many "coincidences" in place and the timeliness of these "graceful interventions" that came to fruition and saved our son's life. He suffered an injury while out of the country.

He made it stateside to a hospital within an hour of his death. He lay in a foreign clinic that was ill-equipped to manage the injury. His friends were advised to get him back to the States for treatment immediately. However, payment needed to be made before the authorities would release him. Unfortunately, his credit card and his friend's credit card did not process in a foreign country. That is when his friends called to notify my husband and me of the accident. We immediately submitted our information only to discover that our credit card was also rejected. His friends looked in our son's wallet once more and found another credit card, which was processed and allowed release. Our son later said he had no idea why he opened a second credit card, as he did not rely on credit cards. I believe that was divine intervention, preparing for what was to come.

He met one of the friends he traveled with three months before the trip. His friend's mom had previously arranged emergency transfers to the border, which accelerated services. She worked stateside to make provisions for the border, followed by an ambulance transfer to the helicopter. The helicopter brought him to a level one trauma center, and according to the doctor, he arrived within an hour of death. Again, I believe what may be called a "coincidence" was divine intervention. God had the right people in place to expedite services that saved our son's life. By the grace of God, his life was spared. *"We appeal to you not to receive the grace of God in vain," 1 Corinthians 6:1*

REFLECTION

1) Do I realize the power of God's grace working in my life? How do I see His grace manifested?

2) Do I refer to God's grace to discern, forgive, or counsel others?

3) Does my ego sometimes take credit for God's grace?

4) Do I acknowledge God's grace and praise and thank Him for the graces bestowed upon myself and others?

"Children, let no one deceive you." (1 John 3:7)

GRACE'S OPPONENT AND CHOICE

The forces of darkness are always tugging and fighting for our souls. God stands graciously and readily available to give you an escape from the allure of evil and temptation, but it may not be as simple as it sounds. God knows and wants the best for you, but His gentle kindness will never force you into His court. The choice is up to you.

Visualize your arms outstretched to each side. Now imagine the forces of God's grace and His righteousness strongly tugging at one arm as God wants you to come into His court. Imagine another force that is bad with evil temptation and the devil tugging on your other arm with every bit of his power in the opposite direction. Both God and the devil badly want you to choose their court. It is up to you. All you must do is shift your weight the slightest, and your choice determines whether you choose good or evil, the straight and narrow road or the broad path that leads to destruction. Your will reflects whether you accept or refuse grace. Which way are you shifting? *"For just as through the disobedience of one person many were made sinners, so through the obedience of one many will be made righteous," (Romans 5:19).* Jesus was obedient to the Father unto death.

In watching the movie "The Passion," I recall how the devil lurked in the background, waiting to attack where one is most vulnerable. That is how Satan works. In *2 Peter 5:8, Peter warns, "Be sober and vigilant. Your opponent, the devil, is prowling around like a roaring lion looking for someone to devour."* He works with subtleties. He knows how to chip away at our sense of right and wrong, downplay wrongdoing, and cleverly manipulate our thoughts so that we don't think wrongdoing is as bad as it is. He can even make us feel entitled to act immorally. We have all witnessed someone justify getting wasted or engaging in reckless behavior after stressful circumstances. It is unpopular in our culture to refer to the devil, and truthfully, I do not want to give him any attention, but it is equally important to bring awareness to God's love and the devil's evilness, both coexisting. Still, God has given us the gift of conscience to distinguish between good and evil.

Whereas Christ brings knowledge to reveal the truth, Satan loves ignorance and manipulates the truth for his agendas. When we learn and exercise our faith and truth, we become a threat to the devil, as it is harder for him to deceive us. At the same time, Christ gives hope and builds us up with grace to strengthen, empower, and steer us to accomplish His will.

REFLECTION

1) How aware of good and evil am I?

2) What "Tugs of War" do I currently experience in my life? What can I do to choose Christ?

3) What does this Bible passage mean? "At the time, all discipline seems a cause not for joy but for pain, but later it brings the peaceful fruit of righteousness to those who are trained by it." *Hebrews 12:11*

4) In what concrete way can I discipline myself to become an open receptacle for Christ's grace?

"All scripture is inspired by God and is useful for teaching, for refutation, for correction, and training in righteousness, so that the one who belongs to God may be competent, equipped for every good work." (2 *Timothy* 3:16-17)

WHO IS YOUR AUTHORITY?

In *Matthew 21:23-27*, the chief priests and elders approached Jesus as He was teaching and said, *"By what authority are you doing these things?"* As the story unfolds, it becomes evident that the chief priests and elders were more interested in protecting their agendas and egos than identifying the truth of authority. They were not sincerely open to the truth; instead, they were bound by their defensiveness and political interests. When we have financial concerns, we seek a financial advisor; mechanical problems, a mechanic; not just any financial advisor or mechanic. We pursue skilled, qualified, trustworthy professionals with integrity.

When seeking qualified, skilled counsel, speak to God Himself or those mature in their faith. Strive to live in the truth and be dedicated to learning and living what is revealed in scripture. When tough faith questions arose *(Acts 15:1-6)*, Paul, Barnabas, and others went to Jerusalem to seek counsel from the apostles and presbyters. Jesus asked the Father to consecrate us in the truth and acknowledged that the Word is the truth *(John 17:17)*. In other words, Jesus asked the Father to direct our desires from the secular world's messages and protect us under God's dominion, the truth revealed through reading scripture. Many walk away from the Catholic faith after seeking answers from ill-formed Catholics who knowingly or unknowingly distort the truth and people of other faiths, instead of adults educated in their Catholic faith. Some people have left the faith without adult catechesis, basing judgment on childhood understandings or misinformation from faltering Catholics.

The Bible repeatedly references Jesus as our Shepherd. In *Ezekiel 34*, our Lord addresses the lack of good shepherding and shepherds who did not look after their sheep while "pasturing themselves," thus leaving the weak, sick, and strayed unattended and scattered. This partially explains our social divides with poverty, addictions, and diversity. In our own way, we, as leaders or laypersons, disconnect from those suffering from pain and turn a blind eye to their needs even though they are entrusted to us by God. We choose to ensure our own comfort over that of the afflicted. Nobody is immune to God's call; even if we are not chosen to be religious or civic leaders, God has given each of us the responsibility of shepherding His sheep in faith, virtue, and love. God has appointed authorities throughout history to impart truth to the masses, but we are responsible for encouraging each other in righteousness and love. Christians are called to learn, seek Godly counsel, and encourage one another according to God's principles.

Seek advice from people of integrity who have the courage to speak truthfully. Unfortunately, we sometimes allow pride to overshadow the truth of our humanity. In our defensiveness or pride, we can become trapped in protecting our agenda and remain closed when listening to someone else. Self-honesty and introspection are imperative in counseling and choosing an advisor. Good Christian counsel incorporates virtues according to the fullness of the truth and encourages integrity. Secular human authorities all have flaws. Parents, educators, politicians, lawyers, business leaders, and priests, to name a few, have and will abuse authority. Flawed leadership has caused brokenness and injustice in the world. We have all been abused by authority or abused authority, even though it is against our standard principles.

What is your reference point for counseling others? *"Speak the truth, each one to his neighbor, for we are members one of another," (Ephesians 4:25).* Does your spiritual counsel guide others in the right direction and coincide with your faith values and virtues? It is important to always set an example by encouraging others and bringing Christian values into your conversations and advice. Not to imply phony piety, which is sometimes confused by worldly messages. The discussion does not have to include a lot of "God-talk," but a Christian witness lives the message. Virtue is attractive. The more it is formed in faith, the more apparent it may be recognized. Civil laws change, but God's Truth does not change. A disciple wants to bear good fruit. *"A good tree does not bear rotten fruit, nor does a rotten tree bear good fruit." A good person, out of the store of goodness in his heart, produces good, but an evil person, out of the store of evil, produces evil; from the fullness of the heart, the mouth speaks," (Luke 7:43, 45).* A formed, conscious matter to one's life responses.

In *Matthew 14*, Herod, delighted by Herodias's daughter's dance, swore to give her whatever she desired. The daughter, "prompted by her mother," asked her father, "Give me here on this platter the head of John the Baptist." Shocked but prideful, Herod gave orders to fulfill the request. The daughter's authority figures betrayed her when they responded out of their sinful natures. The authorities, centered on selfish interests, directed the daughter to react inappropriately. One might ask why the daughter complied with the order. Her life was full of corruption, dishonesty, selfishness, and manipulation, which made it hard for her to see the truth. Her life was controlled by oppressive authoritarians who denied her free speech and independent thinking. She possibly sensed the truth, but the "cost" of rebuking the authorities was too high. We do not have the answer, but we see selfish social and political injustices mimicked throughout history and recognize how one generational action influences subsequent generations. God's Holy Scriptures say that authoritative people have been given the gift of leadership and must respond with grace.

There have been times throughout my life when I sought counsel, knowing the listener would support my stance and tell me what I wanted to hear. Instead, they justified my anger, unforgiving attitude, and negativity, which reinforced my cause to be angry and hold onto my grudge. At other times, cowardly, I shrank and failed to proclaim the truth boldly. I downplayed and sugar-coated it. I did not respond due to my weakness. Maturity and wisdom have taught me to confide in reliable sources who speak honestly. Christ-centered counsel challenges my perspectives, offers constructive criticism, and loves me through their direction. I purposely strive to continue to grow in the boldness of the truth. I depend on spiritual directors and friends established in their faith to serve as suitable counsel and spiritual growth authorities.

REFLECTION

1) Who are my authorities? Do I seek counsel from well-formed sources, or do I take the route of a minimalist?

2) Have I made a small commitment to educating myself about my faith, that I may be a source grounded in the truth?

3) Can I identify people in my life who counsel with honesty, integrity, and courage to speak according to Christian values? Do I recognize people who fear losing favor with me and respond accordingly to what they know I want to hear?

4) What is my reference point in counseling others?

5) Reflect on authoritative figures in your life. Did they exude love, patience, openness, gentleness, concern, compassion, or were they oppressive, critical, domineering, and closed-minded? How did authority influence you positively or negatively?

"Just as a branch cannot bear fruit on its own unless it remains on the vine, so neither can you unless you remain in me. I am the vine; you are the branches. Whoever remains in me and I in him will bear much fruit, because without me you can do nothing." (John 15:4-5)

Have You Tweeted God Today?

Tweeting, blogging, emailing, texting, Instagram, radio, television broadcasts, and other outside influences saturate our culture and influence our decisions. While none of these modes are bad in and of themselves, they are distractions at times and hinder us from conversing with God consistently. A conversation with Jesus is a pipeline to prayer with our Heavenly Father. It can be time spent in silence with God or lifting one's heart and mind to God. Our entire day can become a prayer. God wants us to be in constant communion with Him. This does not mean to drop out of life and be on our knees all day, but to invite God into our daily lives. *"With all prayer and supplication, pray at every opportunity in the Spirit," (Ephesians 6:18).* God is always present to us. Our prayer opens us to Him and helps unite our attention and efforts to His will.

Praying to God should not be a burden but a light to enlighten our day. Have you ever tried to do something in the dark or without your glasses? Our efforts are more efficient with the proper light or clear vision when properly wearing eyeglasses. The same is true of prayer. When we allow God to take control, we allow Him to bring clarity, direction, and guidance to us. He intercedes for those we lift in prayer. Just as we have the awareness to share a tweet with friends and followers, we have the same ability to share Jesus with those we present to Him. Prayer sustains us and helps us reveal God through our daily words and actions. Prayer takes discipline.

"At the time, all discipline seems a cause, not for joy but for pain, but later it brings the peaceful fruit of righteousness to those who are trained by it." (Hebrews 12:11)

DISCIPLINE REQUIRES SACRIFICE

Often, looking at someone's accomplishments appears attainable because you have not witnessed the discipline that has taken place to achieve the result. All discipline requires sacrifice. We discipline ourselves to study for tests, train to become athletes, and attend skill training classes to advance in the workplace. What about our spiritual disciplines? Some neglect discipline and become callous when ignoring the required sacrifice. A genuine relationship requires discipline by investing time with one another to become acquainted. So, it is with God! If we want to know Him, we need to invest time with Him to learn how He speaks to us. We must discipline ourselves to read the scriptures, study, and dedicate time to God in prayer. Jesus reminds us, *"I am the vine, you are the branches," (John 15:4).* By staying connected to Jesus, the vine, we get spiritual nourishment and the strength we need to bear good fruit as his disciples.

Peacefulness is the fruit of a life integrated with God through prayer. With God at the center of all our activity, even the storms become manageable and tolerable. The disciplined one hastens to surrender everything to God and experiences consolation, even as they wait in hopefulness. Scripture encourages and says, *"Have no anxiety at all, but in everything, by prayer and petition, with thanksgiving, make your requests known to God. Then the peace of God that surpasses all understanding will guard your hearts and minds in Jesus Christ," (Philippians 4:6-7).*

PRAYING WITH EXPECTATION

The memory is etched in my mind of when our son endured days of excruciating pain while battling leukemia. My body collapsed across the kitchen table weeks after he was hospitalized. I told God sternly, "You have to do something. I cannot keep this up!" I agonized over our son. I was exasperated and needed help now! I was weak and at the same time had little faith while trusting God. I wanted relief and healing for our son! We entered his hospital room two hours later, and our son was sitting up in bed, smiling and talking with a visitor. For days prior, he was too sick to visit with others. I will never forget how God answered my demanding prayer. I realize some may label this "a coincidence," but I give God the glory. I know He listens. I have witnessed countless answered prayers, and at this time in my life, He taught me to trust and pray with expectant faith. Speak honestly to God. He knows your thoughts. Be candid. Use your heartfelt words and express yourself according to your need.

I read and meditated on the following with confident expectation: *"Ask in faith, not doubting," (James 1:6).* The scriptures are filled with God-inspired people who reach out to Jesus in faith, expecting change. We may all be familiar with the woman with the hemorrhage. She knew if she could get close enough to touch the tassel of Jesus' cloak, she would be healed. She exercised her faith to become cured of her affliction. The man who petitioned Jesus to cast the demonic spirit out of his son knew Jesus had the power. Jesus rewarded the man's act of faith by healing his son. A deaf man with a speech impediment was taken to Jesus and asked Jesus to lay hands on him. Jesus healed the man in response to their expectant faith. Blind Bartimaeus cried out to Jesus in a crowd, asking Jesus to "Have pity on me." He had faith that Jesus had the power to heal, and he expected results with Jesus' blessing. Jesus asked, *"What do you want me to do for you?" The blind man said, "Master, I want to see," (Mark 10:48-52).* He, too, was cured by his act of faith.

PRAY WITH OBEDIENCE AND EXPECTATION

Through His name, Jesus gives us access and authority. He said, *"Whoever believes in me will do the works that I do and will do greater ones than these. If you ask anything of me in my name, I will do it," (John 14: 12-14).* The Bible instructs us to come to Jesus in faith and make our request in His name. We are to do the same works as Jesus. Call upon the Holy Spirit to accomplish great results through your acts of faith. Trust the Holy Spirit to answer. Prayer is often made without a confident expectation that God hears and answers. *"Ask, and you will receive; seek, and you will find; knock, and the door will be opened to you. For everyone who asks receives; the one who seeks finds; and to the one who knocks, the door will be opened," (Luke 11: 9-10).* Listen for the response, but most importantly, trust the Holy Spirit to respond to your ask, knock, and seek in every prayer.

It is imperative to know the voice of God. He speaks in unimaginable ways. God was speaking to me through my desires. I considered initiating a community program, Room at the Inn (RATI), for the homeless at our parish. I wrestled with self-doubt and fear of commitment. A thought entered my mind, "Does God really want me to do this? No one asked me to start the program." I turned on the television to catch the evening news that very evening, which is not typical for me. The supervisor of the RATI volunteers was promoting the program and seeking more volunteers to host night sites. I could have chucked the call as "coincidence," but truthfully, I discerned God was calling me to start the program at our parish. I imagined myself homeless; a safe shelter with dinner, a clean bed, and breakfast would matter to me every day. I forged ahead in obedience to execute God's plan. At times while coordinating the program, apprehensiveness constantly harassed me to give up, but I knew Jesus would never give up on the homeless. I was called to stretch myself in obedience. *"Do to others whatever you would have them do to you," (Matthew 7:12).* I made conscious efforts to pray for the program and surrender my fears to God. After all, God is the power that makes things happen, not me. My mind immediately recalled the multiplication of the loaves of bread in *(John 6:1-15).* Jesus provided the miracle, and the disciples worked up a sweat feeding the five thousand. They refused to remain immobile, got involved, and worked with Jesus. They offered what they had to give, just as worldwide volunteers and RATI local volunteers do to assist the homeless and others in need.

DISCERNING GOD'S VOICE

One means of God's communication is through dreams. When our son was sick, God spoke to me through prophetic dreams. In one dream, I was in a concentration camp, shoulder to shoulder with a mob of people. Someone started passing out pro-abortion badges and demanding that we wear the badge. I was shocked to see so many in compliance. I slid my badge into my pocket, thinking, "Jesus said we will have to suffer persecution for the kingdom of heaven." Upon waking, I understood our cross was part of our journey to salvation.

One Saturday morning, I was torn between being at the hospital with our son, who was going through an exceedingly distressful time, and the need to be with our other children for their activities. Before I awoke, I dreamt I put a piece of paper in a Xerox machine. An extremely bright light lit up with the words "Be Patient." I knew that it was a message from God. All morning, while I accompanied our children to their activities, I rested patiently in God, knowing He was in control and taking care of matters. Late that afternoon, I visited our son. Sure enough, the doctor was steps ahead of me when I entered the hospital. I was there in time to hear the results of the infectious disease report, indicating matters were stabilized. God's message on patience carried me through the morning while the angels of the Lord protected our son.

In another dream, I looked up into the night sky while camping with my family and saw a gigantic angel overseeing all of us. I said to my children, "Look how huge that angel is from here! Imagine how much protection He is providing us!" It was a great reminder that angels surround us and protect us through everything, even in our current drudgeries. I have received countless messages conveyed through dreams and mention them to remind listeners that God speaks in numerous ways. As you lay your head down each night, give Him your thoughts and your entire being. God speaks in various ways.

God spoke to me while reading Francis McNutt's book, Healing. I undoubtedly believed in the power of prayer, my call to pray with expectant faith, and that prayers effect outcomes, even to the extent of miracles. Even though healing prayer ministry was out of the box for me, I felt compelled to contact our local Catholic Renewal Center to discuss this fervent desire to pray and be prayerfully present to others for healing. I never proclaim to have the healing power of Jesus Christ, but I know we can all be instruments of God's healing power for others when we pray with expectant faith and allow the Holy Spirit to work in our lives. In scripture, we repeatedly see the power of Jesus' healing touch. When we respectfully touch and pray with or over one another, we, too, are an extension of Jesus. It is Jesus who imparts healing.

God speaks through our imagination when praying. We can visualize presenting a person or matter to God. We must entrust God to answer our most intimate prayers. Imagine yourself as a person in a scripture passage: the prodigal son, his elder brother, or his father. Imagine clinging to the foot of the cross, or Jesus embracing you or another and holding you to his loving heart. Then imagine God's grace pouring over you. Imagine God answering that specific prayer you presented to Him. Receive it!

Journaling is an effective way to communicate with God. Before journaling, embrace a feeling or meditate on a word or passage from scripture that captures your heart and mind. Be honest when you write down what comes to mind. Typically, as I record thoughts, the conversation turns to God. The words penned onto the page suddenly become directed at me rather than God, as the Holy Spirit answers, guides, enlightens me to see from another perspective, and challenges me to action. In journaling, write freely without regard to style; the important thing is to record thoughts, feelings, and inspirations revealed during the experience. Listen, record, and contemplate how the message applies to your personal life.

God is good, and He wants the very best for all of us! Allow Him to envelop you and place His desires within you. Bask in His serenity, love, and consolation. It is all yours. It is His gift to you. Remember to stay connected and "tweet" Him throughout your day. Always listen with expectant faith!

Be silent and relax in the presence of God each day. If you are just initiating the discipline, start with ten-minute increments of prayer. Make a conscious decision to sit with Him silently. Communicate with words or no words, be with Him and honor Him with your dedicated stillness. There are God-given creative ways to develop habitual prayer relationships; set your alarm; record notes; and set out a rosary or bible. Start simply and recommit to God when you forget to show up to pray.

REFLECTION

1) Do I dedicate time for silent prayer with God?

2) How does discipline play out in my prayer life?

3) Do I converse with God throughout my day, uniting my day with Him?

4) How does God communicate with me personally?

5) Do I pray with expectant faith?

"Sanctify yourselves then, to be holy; for I, the Lord, your God, am holy. Be careful, therefore, to observe what I, the Lord, who makes you holy, have prescribed." (Leviticus 20:7-8)

HOLINESS

God made us in His image, and He resides within us when we surrender to His holiness. We must allow God to peel off the layers that mask and awaken holiness. Sometimes, people's perception of holiness appears to be too noble, too pious, or unachievable and is only for the saints. Yes, it is for the saints, but we are all called to sainthood. Study the lives of the saints, and it becomes apparent quickly that many were sinners like us, with examples of similar spiritual battles, but in uniting their souls to Christ, they grew in holiness. We are called to the same task: to tie everything to Christ, including our attitudes, feelings, joys, and hard work.

Holiness is a necessary process for salvation. God intends to use each one of us to lead others to Him.

Eternal salvation is our goal. The other option is eternal damnation. God doesn't desire for anyone to experience eternal damnation. God's will is for everyone to spend eternity with Him. Jesus shows us how to live and die in union with the Father. This is the perfect example of holiness. He loves sinners equally as His followers. In love and compassion, He extends himself to the poor, isolated, and forgotten. He healed spiritual, mental, and physical illnesses. He cast out demons, forgave sinners, loved everyone, promoted justice, and even showed us how to suffer persecution united to the Father. He always prayed and executed the Father's will. He was kind and gentle, nonjudgmental, generous, merciful, and tender. In His humanity, Jesus experienced pain, suffering, isolation, hatred, and all human emotions. Holiness commands that we take up our human experiences and emotions, whatever messes, crosses, loneliness, disgruntled trying times, and bring them to God to heal and comfort. He disperses grace. Holiness sincerely gives praise and thanks to God for everything and seeks to genuinely be the face of Christ to those whom Christ places in our path each day.

Read and meditate on scripture as Jesus instructs in holiness. Christ gives us a moral code to *"Live by the Spirit, and you will certainly not gratify the desires of the flesh. For the flesh has desires against the Spirit, and the Spirit against the flesh; these are opposed one to each other so that you may not do what you want," (Galatians 5:17). "The works of the flesh are "immorality, impurity, licentiousness, idolatry, sorcery, hatreds, rivalry, jealousy, outbursts of fury, acts of selfishness, dissensions, factions, and occasions of envy, drinking bouts, orgies, and the like," (Galatians 5:16-17, 19).* But those who live by the Spirit receive the fruits of the Spirit: *"love, joy, peace, patience, kindness, generosity, faithfulness, gentleness, and self-control," (Galatians 5:22-23)* as a reward for denying their flesh."

Holiness is attainable through prayer, meditating on scripture, and surrendering our ways to follow Christ's way. *"He must increase; I must decrease," (John 3:30).* When we submit everything, even our small ways, to Christ, he increases within us, and we begin to live by the Spirit rather than gratifying the desires of the flesh.

Fasting increases the soul's power over the flesh. Ignore the desire to satisfy the flesh when abstaining, no matter how loud and persistent the cravings nag at you. Instead, focus on the Spirit that yearns for unity with God. I have noted great consolation when I prayerfully succeed in fasting. It's not easy, but it's a beautiful way to connect with Jesus. Through fasting and prayer, we gain spiritual strength. In essence, we invite God to increase within us; when God increases, we grow in holiness. St. Paul speaks of "perfect maturity" in Christ as a "pursuit in hope," as *"straining forward to what lies ahead and the goal, the prize of God's upward calling," (Philippians*

3:12-13). Paul stretches himself in pursuit of reaching his goal of maturing in his relationship with Christ. We have the same option of stretching ourselves and growing into an appropriate relationship with Christ or remaining stagnant. Growth entails enduring temptation. Even Jesus was tried through temptations. Yet, God recognizes our obedience, and we grow in holiness as we align our will with God's.

Jesus stretches us beyond our capabilities. He strategically allows us to experience messy life events to become the platform for healing and spiritual growth. At one point in life, I had to face a deep hurt. I furiously hated the person who betrayed me. I could not believe how much I hated. I envisioned relief and no remorse at the thought of the person's death. My body shuddered when I spoke in confidence about the offense against me. God gave me a new vision as I brought the situation to Him in prayer and worked diligently with a spiritual counselor. He helped me see that one person's sin held me in bondage to self-hatred, shame, guilt, hatred of another, unforgiveness, and victimhood. This all became fertile ground for me to grow in holiness. Through persistent prayer, God began to soften my heart and show me the truth that lay beneath the sin that was inflicted upon me.

CONFRONTING FEELINGS

First, I recognized His love, constant presence, strength, and healing power flowing as I reached out for healing and help. Second, I began to understand the cycle of evil. The sin inflicted upon me resulted from the sin imposed upon my perpetrator. Not to make excuses and dismiss evil. Yes, evil happens when we hurt each other, but God's grace revealed I could cooperate to halt the cycle. Third, I learned to forgive and love the person despite their culpability through prayer and God's power. I had a choice; to wrap myself in self-pity and anger and continue to feel victimized or accept God's mercy and use His grace for life-giving freedom. It took consistent effort, but through God's mercy, my hard shell softened. As my attitudes transformed, I began to see the love and goodness in the perpetrator by discovering that the evil act that they committed did not define them. I learned to love and forgive others more eagerly and judge less. I am much less inclined to hold others to judgment. I now understand our past has an impact on our present reactions. I love myself and others more freely, possess deeper trust in God, understand inner wounds, and desire healing for others. I want everyone to know God's love and healing power! God bestows abundant blessings upon those who carry their suffering with Him. Illuminated with a new spirit, one can better serve as His instrument of holiness, His hands, feet, and heart in the world.

Walking through the coals of hatred to forgiveness, God brought me to freedom and taught me to become holier. Align everything, even the most hidden and mundane, with His heart and allow His mercy to bring light and transformation. We have a practical Jesus. He meets us where we are and invites us into His heart through our joys and conflicts, the messes of our lives. Yes, new messes and opportunities for perfecting holiness are continually present throughout life. Whether it be a deep hurt or a simple surrender, life is full of opportunities to gain knowledge. Our final victory is through holiness.

REFLECTION

1) What are your beliefs regarding holiness?

2) What experience can you invite God into at this moment, i.e., joy, fear, bitterness, anger, etc.? Can you speak candidly to Him or hand over the situation for Him to shine His Light upon?

3) Do you think of yourself as being an instrument for Christ or being the face of Christ to others?

4) Who is the face of Christ to you?

"Faith is the realization of what is hoped for, and evidence of things not seen." (Hebrews 11:1)

FAITH COMMUNITY

What is your definition of faith? We are taught to believe and trust even though we do not fully understand or know the outcome. So, likewise, it is with faith in God. Logic often defies what God asks of us, but in faith, one knows, believes, and trusts that God, in His infinite wisdom, knows best. God has left us with excellent examples of faith in the Bible.

I began to understand faith through life experiences and the many illustrations in the Bible. As a parent consumed with anxiety and worry, it takes great faith to let go, surrender my child to God, and trust that God will answer my prayer requests according to His will rather than mine. It is possible to maintain the peace of God despite difficulties while awaiting unanswered prayers if we trust in God. Life's challenges give us an opportunity to develop faith and trust in God. Faith can be challenged from moment to moment as we vacillate in and out of faithfully trusting in God. God allows numerous occasions to develop faith.

Sometimes it is hard to see God's goodness while He is working during life's most difficult sufferings. Our daughter questioned how her brother's suffering from leukemia positively affected our family. Truthfully, I pondered the same question and had difficulty seeing the positive impact. However, I constantly recognized God's goodness in the countless people who prayed and supported us through our suffering. While I was carrying my cross, Christ's disciples were there for me to help me through the storms and battles of life.

The unexpected diagnosis filled our family with sorrow, fear, anxiety, and emptiness. Having lost a nine-year-old brother to aplastic anemia, a rare form of leukemia, and more recently, a young nephew to cancer, the implications of a leukemia diagnosis dislodged frightening memories. We were not equipped to handle the trial, but God's grace gave us the strength to endure the suffering. Our faith was tested to new levels, and years later, I understood the positives that came from our trial. Even though much brokenness seemed to stem from the challenge, in hindsight, brokenness existed already, undetected, and the illness exposed our weaknesses, lack of faith, hope, and trust in God. What a gift and seeds for growth!

When diagnosed with leukemia, our son was seemingly at a high point in life. The unexpected diagnosis brought disappointment and sorrow. Within forty-five minutes after our son was admitted to the hospital, the nurse entered the room with an IV to administer medication to prepare his kidneys for chemotherapy. We were shocked to start chemotherapy that soon! Although I was not present, I have sad, piercing memories of my husband returning home from the hospital at three o'clock in the morning to be with our other three children when they awoke. Our daughter came downstairs, apprehensive when she heard her dad crying. She had not yet slept, fearing for her brother. Fear intensified due to losing our nephew, who was our sick son's age, just two years earlier, to bone cancer. Our faith and hope were tested again.

One night, overcome with sadness, my husband and I lay in bed together. We had nothing to offer each other but tears and grief. It felt miserable not to have anything to offer. It was apparent how deeply we loved our children and each other. It hurt immensely to see our son suffer while trying to hold it together. We were unequipped to emotionally support each other and our other children, especially our daughter, who seemed highly aware of the seriousness of the disease. Our only hope was in God and His ability to provide healing to our son.

We often read and hear that God provides, and He does! He continually surrounded us with His love, compassion, and presence. The generous outpouring of love and care through family, friends, acquaintances, and the medical team aroused overwhelming appreciation and support. It became an opportunity for me to remind our children of God's presence and provisions. As messy as it was in our time of need, God was holding us together. Prayer warriors were pounding heaven's gates for us. Family, friends, and people all over the globe lifted us in prayer. The love and support increased my strength to bear the load.

I had many powerful lessons in prayer throughout the challenge. I prayed a nine-hour novena to St. Michael of the Saints, a patron saint of cancer patients. Initially, I placed my petition with God to heal our son. Before concluding my prayer, I surrendered our son to God, trusting that He knew what was best for his soul. My prayer changed to, "Lord, you know my will, but You know what is best for our son's soul. If it is Your will for him to be here on this earth for a brief time, I ask for the strength to go forward in your will. May he live to glorify you if your will aligns with mine!" Thank God our son recovered. Although he has encountered struggles in the following years, peace prevails when I refer to the promises made in that prayer. I know God listens and has a plan for our son, His child. I attended a prayer healing service at our parish that strengthened my faith and helped me see God's plan unfold in the future. I invited another mom whose son had a blood condition to attend the prayer service. Her son had fought the disorder for years, and his medical prognosis gave little hope that he would outgrow it. She had not considered attending the healing service but changed her mind after listening to my suggestion. The prayer service was simple. Each sick person was presented for prayer, and all who cared could come forward and lay their hand on the sick person to extend healing blessings. Family and friends gathered around our son to offer blessings, and some of us stayed for the other child and laid hands on him. I felt much hope.

Laying hands was powerful! I remember returning to our seats, amazed by the power I felt in the prayer service. Years later, recollection of that experience seeded personal understanding, faith, and a passion to pray with others. When we prayerfully hold hands or lay hands, we yoke with Jesus through touch and become an extension of Him.

Our son had additional complications that increased his risk of healing. When he was sick, burdened with worry, I recalled the powerful healing prayer service and trusted in the grace gifted through it, the St. Michael novena, and everyone's prayers. The memories provided comfort, peace, and hope while going through my trial. I knew our son may have been healed but had to continue with treatment. God heard our prayers and answered them according to His will. For the first time in my prayer life, I started to understand praying with confidence and expectation – the faithful expectation that God hears, listens, and provides. Jesus says, "*Have faith in God. Amen, I say to you, whoever says to this mountain, "Be lifted up and thrown into the sea" and does not doubt in his heart but believes that what He says will happen, it shall be done to him. Therefore, I tell you, all that you ask for in prayer, believe that you will receive it, and it shall be yours" (Mark 11: 22-24).* I realized that both our son and the other child were healed from their diseases. God gave them special graces that evening, and I live in gratitude for all the prayers murmured on our behalf. I know every prayer is answered, even when the answer or the results are unparalleled to our desires. I know now that seeds of healing were planted in preparation for my involvement with prayer ministry. I believe and witness the power of prayer!

Throughout years of illness, fear and distrust dictated many of our feelings. Our daughter, like me, was riddled with anxiety, having just lost a cousin to cancer and seeing her parents frazzled with fear. Our relationship became incompatible, like oil and water; emotions raged, and communication never seemed to get to the source of the problems. One day, as she left for school, we were upset and screaming at each other. It was against my will to separate on bad terms if something terrible happened; I never want anyone to live with regret over their last words to each other. God used our tumultuous relationship to help me grow in virtue. Typically, I bantered about aggravating situations in my head all day, preparing my defense. Instead, I practiced silencing negative, unproductive thoughts and prayed about the problem. I will never forget our daughter's most loving greeting as she returned home from school and the tremendous outpouring of love God bestowed upon me. It changed my life forever. The conflict was a nonissue, and God restored our attitudes by His grace. Prayer works! And so does virtue! My faith increased. By the grace of God, silencing my thoughts and praying instead has become a habitual practice that results in better communication, a mature temperament, and a peaceful relationship. Yesterday's trials were the seeds for today's faith, courage, and love.

My faith was strengthened when I suffered through my trials. Jesus taught me that I lack faith and hope but empowered me in my weakness. Life became more peaceful as I traded anxiety and fears for faithful trust in God's Divine Providence, but I also learned lessons on hope.

REFLECTION

1) Do I possess expectant faith? When I pray, does God hear, listen, and answer?

2) Am I trained to listen, "hear," and see answers to prayers?

3) Is there a particular time I felt especially tested in faith? If so, how did that experience affect my relationship with God?

4) Do I respond with faithful trust in God and make decisions accordingly?

5) Make one commitment to act in faith today.

"... but we even boast of our afflictions, knowing that affliction produces endurance, and endurance, proven character, and proven character, hope, and hope does not disappoint." (Romans 5: 3-5)

HOPE

As a mother consumed with worry, fear rocked my peace. I feared something would happen to my children, especially during their teenage years, when lessons regarding friendship, responsibility, peer pressure, obedience, and rebellion have many harsh consequences. While they had their lessons, I, too, had lessons to learn including trusting God with this area of my life! Their activities often created growing pains. As I brought my anxieties and frustrations to God, I began to recognize how little I trusted God with my children. Although my trust had grown in the past decade, He brought me to another level of trust and taught me to place my hope in Him.

There was a period when one child was incredibly fragile, which caused me to worry constantly. One night, I had a dream. I was in a beautiful church ground setting, around a lake with gorgeous green, succulent vegetation. Everything about it was gorgeous and peaceful. Everyone present was joyful and peaceful, except me. I was worried about an issue, just like in real life. When I awoke and applied it to my life, I realized that worry robs us of happiness, peace, and faith. It kept me bound in hopelessness. The root of worry comes from fear and a lack of trust in God, which parallels a lack of hope. With hope, I pray with expectation and leave it in God's hands, entrusting the matter to Him. My consolation is peace.

Learning to trust and hope took substantial perseverance and practice for me. Every day I entrusted my family to God, reciting the following prayer:

Letting Go Prayer

In Your Care and Keeping

Author unknown

Father, here are my dear ones. (I imagined myself placing each one in His embrace). I place them lovingly in your care. I trust your spirit in them. I trust your light shining within them to make clear and plain the way before them. Father, I know your infinite plan of good for them is unfolding. I may not see how the sometimes-tangled affairs in their lives will work out, but I trust in your loving spirit at work in and through them to make all things right. I am willing to release worry and anxiety about my dear ones. I am willing to release preconceived notions as to what they should do or how they should conduct their lives. I am willing to trust your spirit in them. I know that in ways beyond my power to imagine and in ways far greater than my personal wishes for them, you are blessing them.

On multifold days, I had to repeat the prayer numerous times throughout the day, as my tendency to worry overpowered any amount of hope within. Over time and by God's grace, I learned to trust in the prayerful words murmured. When doubts and worries resurface after prayer now, I remember the matter was placed in God's hands earlier; I give it back to Him with expectant faith and trust and place my hope in the Lord. It is difficult to surrender and trust when trust has been destroyed but pray with expectant faith and hope. If difficult, practice the virtue of hope, and know that God cares. Surrender to Him, and His peace prevails. God knows our concerns; our job is to trust and hope in God. Faith, hope, and trust interweave to aid us in our afflictions.

Prayers muttered without hope resemble babble. Pray with trust and confidence, exercise hope, and know that God's answer lies on the horizon. I learned to react less to teenagers' early-stage plans and to pray more instantly. My "wedge prayer," as I called it, brought me peace. "Lord, if it is not within your will, please place a wedge in the plan." Hope softened worry.

God often presents the smallest piece of evidence as a sign of hope. A friend going through horrible marital issues confided in me. Constantly, God amazed me! As terrible as her situation was, the Holy Spirit seemed to shine a ray of light on the tiniest thread of evidence to encourage hope and direct specific prayer for her need. The friend persevered in love and hopeful prayer and worked on self-transformation to strengthen the marriage despite the spouse's actions. She trusted in the midst of adversity with faithful trust and hope in God, who spared the marriage in the end. Without hope, she could have easily walked out on what God healed.

Hope presents itself in the person who loves another despite years of unreciprocated love or in the person who prays for an enemy, an addict, a marriage, the grieving, isolated, persecuted, mentally afflicted, etc. Hope reigns in the person who prayerfully tries to heal from physical, emotional, or spiritual wounds. Hope knows that God hears, listens, and is always on time. The fruit of hope is patience and peace.

A journal entry captures the essence of lessons on hope learned through prayer.

Hope is...

Rooted in Christ

In the waiting

In displacement

In the joyful and sorrowing

In the lonely, poor, and oppressed

In generous reaching out

In a gentle touch

Kind voice

In the comforter and comforted

In our conversations with God

Hope finds a home within:

A mother, father, child, teacher, prisoner, counselor,

laborer seeking love, justice, righteousness

Hope wipes away tears

Conquers fears

Softens worry

Turns darkness to light

Springs forth energy

Soothes discouragement

Breeds optimism

Encourages

Hope depends on trust in God.

Without trust, hope dims.

Help me, Lord, to trust and hope in you!

REFLECTION

1) Do I find it easy to entrust some matters to God but difficult to surrender others? What influences my ability to trust or not trust? Do I exercise hope?

2) What are the fruits of living in hope?

3) How can I stretch myself to grow in hope?

4) Is there a particular situation in my life now that calls for increased hope? If so, how might I respond?

"Beloved, let us love one another because love is of God; anyone who loves is begotten by God and knows God. Whoever is without love is without God, for God is love." (1 John 4:7-8)

LOVE

LOVE! LOVE! LOVE! *"God is love" (1 John 4:8).* He loves me despite my frailties and woundedness; thus, I am to replicate and love my neighbor with the same unconditional love. When tested to love, we are called to love God in everything and everyone! Is it possible to love others with Godly love while someone insults, ridicules, places judgment, ignores, and lacks love and compassion for their neighbor?

What about ISIS? The Taliban? Corrupt political leaders? How do I love human traffickers and those who train children to become Unabombers or abuse vulnerable individuals? God created us in His image, despite the fact that we all have a sinful nature. How do I love unconditionally, much less help another person to love? It is impossible to achieve this type of love without God. But a personal commitment to do God's will on earth can achieve positive results. Scripture is not vague about love. *"Love is patient. Love is kind. It is not jealous, [love] is not pompous, it is not inflated, it is not rude, it does not seek its own interests, it is not quick-tempered, it does not brood over injury, it does not rejoice over wrongdoing but rejoices with the truth. Love bears all things, believes all things, hopes all things, endures all things. Love never fails," (1 Corinthians 13:4-8).*

Seek, pray, and ask God to direct you to love all humanity with the love of Christ. Turn to Jesus to see how He loved the isolated leper, the dishonest tax collector, the sinful woman at the well, the rejected, judged beggar at the gate, and his persecutors who flogged Him, chided Him, abandoned Him, and nailed Him to the cross. Identify with each character and recognize Jesus loved each person and even acknowledged their ignorance, *"Father, forgive them, they know not what they do," (Luke 23:34).* We are called to love the disfigured, the disabled, the outcast, those who cheat, steal, oppose, or persecute us. Like Jesus, we do not have to like the behavior. Still, when we turn to God with our negative thoughts and feelings, we should seek grace to see the person as Jesus sees and loves them. God's love changes our attitudes and opens the way for grace to flow through us like water over pebbles in a stream.

"I give you a new commandment: love one another." As I have loved you, so you also should love one another," (John 13:34). Jesus not only commands us to love others, but also assists us in developing stronger love relationships with our parents, siblings, children, spouse, friends, acquaintances, and strangers. How can we extend our love to others when we allow selfishness, self-hatred, shame, guilt, unforgiveness, laziness, and

other emotions to keep us in bondage? God wants the best for us. To love like God is vital. Invite love to speak to your heart. Lord, show me what the root of my anger is. Why am I so bitter? We can present unlimited unhealthy situations to God. God, who is love, desires to show us how much He loves us, even in our brokenness. God shines the truth at the root of our pain and dysfunction. He speaks forgiveness into our hearts, provides grace to forgive, wisdom, and zeal to respond in love to the needs of others. God loves us and wants us to love ourselves and extend His love to others.

Have you ever felt stuck? I recall a period in life when I had an extremely odd reoccurrence in social situations. The conversation was engaging when suddenly I would shut down. In a flash of a second, I went from being engaged in conversation to withdrawing from the conversation. I felt like a turtle going into its shell. I wanted to go into hiding and not be seen. I felt exposed.

I shut down right away and couldn't open up and talk freely at social gatherings. Frequent occurrences led me to prayer and follow up with counseling. I realized I could only go so far in relationships because I was holding a huge secret and living with shame and guilt. I gained freedom by exposing the humiliating situation to a few trusted friends and confronting the pain. It was unnecessary to announce the incident to the world, but God freed me of the bondage. Reflection revealed dishonesty, low self-esteem, and a lack of confidence. At times, God heals in stages. By giving everything to God, I was able to heal more, gain confidence, and love more honestly and freely, despite my flaws.

I was scared by my father's authoritative nature, which kept me stuck, but with God, I learned to love him despite his inadequacies. His authority was oppressive, but he loved the best he knew how and amazingly well when I consider the lack of love he received from his father. His father did not extend love, a sharp contrast from a dad who truly extended himself lovingly to others. God provided insight, understanding, forgiveness, and healing to move forward. As a young mother, I missed the mark on loving through messes in life when instead, I reacted out of fear. Sometimes, when one of my children made a mistake, I could not convey unconditional love in the moment, which only festered the mess. Prayer exposed my emotions of imperfection. Although my weaknesses are not mastered, I realize healthier responses as God's light has exposed my weaknesses, and His healing grace allows me to love myself better despite imperfections. God imparted compassion, humility, and love through my faults with incredible gifts to pay forward. Now I am more patient with myself and others' sins; slower to judge, and more inclined to love through situations. Inner healing is essential to self-love. Our ultimate goal is to be the authentic person God created us to be in this life. Self-love is the precursor to loving your neighbor. We must first love ourselves and acknowledge and reverence God's presence within itself as a gift! All gifts from God are meant to be shared, and love is the greatest gift of all to share. Love challenges me to evaluate my love and deeds for the poor. How can I eat as much rich, delicious food, junk food, and soda when another person in this world does not have a bowl of rice? How can I love them and join myself in their suffering? I am tested to fast and give small sufferings to God (forgoing a simple indulgence) for their good. Imagine saving the money spent on typical daily luxuries for a year and giving it to the poor. Imagine how awareness of the poor improves if a daily fast draws me to offer prayers for them. My fast was nothing compared to what many people go through, but it has increased my mindfulness and, hopefully, my responses. Then consider the faith dimension of God's grace poured out through fasting. Fasts united to God become prayer, and God, who "sees the hidden"

(Matthew 6:18), reciprocates in abundance. Commit your heart to God. Good friends commit themselves to each other. They are present for each other to give and receive love—commitment roots in relationships. Sometimes selfishness interferes, and we fall short of our love commitment. As we practice uniting our ways with God's ways, it becomes easier to love others, even in challenging situations. Ample opportunities exist each day to love as Jesus loves. Choose love through the mess of life!

Genuine love is attractive. We are all attracted to certain people because of the genuine love, joy, or acceptance they exude. They love generously through their actions. St. Francis of Assisi said, "Preach the gospel at all times and, when necessary, use words."

Anything accomplished in the context of God's love can result in love. God pursues us and blesses us with his love. When our son experienced a traumatic injury while out of the country, fear, anxiety, and extreme sorrow were present; hope, trust, and love were tested at a new level, but God carries us in His infinite love. Friends, family, acquaintances, and our now adult children supported us with immense love, tenderness, and consideration. They were at our side to encourage, bring hope and walk through the coals with us. Sibling love, compassion, and encouragement for a brother in need radiated. God provided the faith that allows me to see, hear, and know His voice. I am grateful for the faith that got us through and calmed our sorrowful hearts. I referred to Our Sorrowful Mother to check my faith as my tears streamed. Did I lack trust? Hope? Was I unable to walk the walk? No, Our Lady cried too when her child, Jesus, was hurt. My tears were justified, and I had to thank God for the gift of our children and for letting me deeply love even though it hurt. What greater gift is there than love?

Four months after the injury, while on retreat, I stole a walk in the cold air just before dusk. Deer wandered in the snow-covered woods as sunlight filtered through the trees. I admired nature and glanced at the river on my right, and in a split second, God chimed in. I glanced quickly to the left, and my eyes fell upon the thirteenth station of the cross – Jesus being taken down from the cross. I saw the love, tenderness, and compassion of all those handling Jesus' lifeless body in that split second. Immediately, God showed me the same love, tenderness, and compassion given to our son in the first hours of his injury when he had little control over his lifeless body. As many prayed from afar after hearing about the injury, God provided for our son's care through all those surrounding him. God broke in when I did not expect it and reminded me of his constant loving presence. Prayer warriors sought his protection in faith, and Jesus delivered. He is with me with the same vigilance. He would always love me. I am grateful for the generosity bestowed upon our family and the Christian community who supported us through a crisis. Love is powerful, and we do not have to be in a crisis to experience God's love. God continuously proves His love to us daily, and we exercise that same love for others. The world needs communities built on love.

REFLECTION

1) Do you believe God, our Creator, loves everyone?

2) Do you love freely or hold back?

3) Is there currently someone who is difficult for you to love? If so, can you commit to praying for the person?

4) How does a weakness, i.e., anger, shame, guilt, greed, etc., hold us in bondage and interfere with loving another unconditionally?

5) God invites everyone to love deeper. Are you disposed to receive his love? Sit silently and be in His presence.

"We must consider how to rouse one another to love and good works. We should not stay away from our assembly, as is the custom of some, but encourage one another..."
(Hebrews 10:24-25)

COMMUNITY

We were not created to operate independently. Diverse communities take on a joint mission to live and work together for the common good. We need each other to encourage, build on one another's talents, critique, and tweak efforts for the community. For example, the medical community shares information and ideas that promote challenges, changes, and analysis. Families are communities that take on a likeness of character, sometimes the same profession, personality, hobbies, and cultural and charitable interests. Communities of musicians in the same genre speak the same language and develop a character that composes a likeness of jazz, blues, hard rock, rock and roll, and gospel music.

Each community holds one another accountable while building an effective and purposeful system. Likewise, faith communities are created to take on Christ's personality and use Christian principles to impact world conditions. Prayers help Christians grow spiritually and teach, enrich, and encourage disciples to go out into the world with courage and spread the gospel.

Diverse personalities within communities help us live with one another. We learn to love through differences, show kindness, consideration, and compassion. The community members hold each other accountable to stretch, accept ourselves, grow in humility, and relinquish self-centered agendas. Likewise, we learn much about ourselves and others; our strengths, weaknesses, hot buttons, leadership potential, obedience, meekness, arrogance, generosity, and critical thinking skills. The list is endless. We learn patterns of behavior and test communication styles. Communities help individuals find and achieve their purpose. We rely on each other's talents and gain from interpersonal exchanges.

It is valuable to seek life experiences that draw out individual giftedness for the glory of God. We need one another's gifts as Christ calls us into the community to complete His works. No one person is single-handedly endowed enough to tackle all the issues in the community without the help of others. Together, we are called to use our gifts to support all of humanity. Contrary to secular world messages, God created us to love and help one another in this life. We need each other to mature emotionally, intellectually, and spiritually.

We are one body that functions with many parts. We are uniquely joined together as members *(1 Corinthians 12-26).* Each person is a part of Christ's body to carry out His purpose *(1 Corinthians 12:27).* We are all part of one body, each having its particular function.

The RATI community day shelter collaborates with organizations within the community to provide a night shelter. The day shelter sets goals with the homeless clients and provides programming to facilitate success. The night shelters provide transportation, dinner, hospitality, lodging, and breakfast. The program exemplifies the Body of Christ in action; administrators, volunteers, and homeless clients work together to combat homelessness, sharing talents, food, and stories. Laughter and joy often fill the atmosphere, and tears of sorrow and fear at other moments. It is an exchange of love between the shelter, the community, and the homeless. Each person brings their gifts to the table, and blessings are present despite the mess and challenges of homelessness.

Homebound individuals often speak of their yearning for community and how they miss worship and parish life. Jesus says, *"Whoever does the will of my heavenly*

Father is my brother, sister, and mother," (Matthew 12:50). He invites all into his holy family to learn and grow in His love. From generation to generation, Jesus called disciples to produce more disciples, and we are his current day disciples. The personal stories above illustrate how we worship in communion and support each other through suffering, sorrows, illness, and stagnant times. We continually study our common faith, seek answers to questions, share spirituality, serve the poor and vulnerable. We hold each other accountable, encourage one another's life with Jesus, and learn the ways of Jesus.

We can speak of human actions within the context of community and forget about the invisible hand of God present in those who show up for Christian worship. Trust that God works in all souls who show up to be with Him. It is not about what "I" do, but what Jesus wants to do with our presence. Some avoid community worship, complaining of boredom or no apparent consolation, not realizing it is not about feelings, but rather about being obediently present to God so that He may act within the soul according to His desires. We may not be aware of the grace bestowed at the moment, but we can trust God's action upon the soul. Our presence pleases Him. God wants communities of Christian disciples to carry on His work. He continuously forms acquiescent souls for His kingdom here on earth. Show up for God.

REFLECTION

1) What communities are you involved in? What do you share?

2) What is the personality of a community you reflect upon? Is it life-giving?

3) Are you actively involved in a community that fosters a relationship with Jesus?

In all circumstances give thanks, for this is the will of God for you in Christ Jesus." (1Thessalonians 5:17)

GRATITUDE

The Eucharist means thanksgiving (CCC 1360), which focuses on gratitude. It is natural to thank God for the pleasantries of life. Quite the contrary, it requires a true exercise of faith to offer my gratitude to God in stormy seasons of life. It seemed beyond my faith limits to appreciate and give thanks for difficult circumstances in life. However, God supplied the grace to understand that gratitude is the greatest antidote to soothing moments of desolation. Sadness lifts, hope mounts, and peace ensues with prayers of gratitude. Even though there is a cross, there are many blessings, and God gives comfort to those who see the blessings in their lives even when there are storms. Turn your eyes away from the storm long enough to glimpse the goodness God presents despite the pain. He will relieve you. He will not necessarily remove the impediment, but He will console you with strength, peace, and hope to get through the hurdle. He will relieve your worry and emptiness. Make a daily commitment to show gratitude to God in good and troubled times to unite the soul with God. Souls connected to God find peace and joy in times of suffering. It takes spiritual muscle to value both suffering and thanksgiving to God in all things. We are made strong through trials. God is our rock. Cling to Him! Praise Him and Thank Him. He will bring you through the storm.

REFLECTION

1) Do you consistently give gratitude to God?

2) Do you struggle to give thanks in times of suffering? Can you see God's presence despite the challenge?

3) Spend a few quiet minutes thanking God or think about writing down the things you're thankful for right now in a journal.

EPILOGUE

This manuscript was born from events that occurred in the mess of life years ago. The messes of life and struggles began when I had childlike faith. My faith grew towards a richer understanding of the theological virtues: faith, hope, and love. Words, which were once concepts, acquired depth as I struggled with complicated circumstances. I value the hardships that unearthed what was in my soul. I am forever grateful for the spiritual insights and realize God will work through my weaknesses until my last breath, but I live in hope, appreciating His movements.

In this era of relativism, individuals frequently determine their own truth, their own way, rather right or wrong. Selfishly, one makes up their own moral guidelines so as not to be accountable to religious or societal rules and policies. Before the transformation, I was guilty of the same behavior and remain on guard to avoid such accommodations. I appreciate that God gave us the Ten

Commandments not to control humankind but rather as a means for humanity to obtain Godly freedom and love. Trust his ways. Be on guard as people manipulate language to force ungodly agendas.

At baptism, baptized into God's grace, we were made ready to see God and grow in virtue. Life events, including suffering, induce growth. Jesus promised at his death that the Holy Spirit would descend and fill the earth with the fire of God's love and truth. The Holy Spirit nudges, invites, guides, and prepares us through life for our eternal victory in heaven. All the joys and afflictions in life, the big and small messes we encounter, all serve as opportunities to dig deeper and find Jesus. Discover what is hidden in the soul and listen to the Spirit. God allows challenges for our growth but never turns his back on us. Be willing to lose everything for God – face vulnerabilities and cast them into God's arms for Him to mold into a higher good and unity with Him. He avails Himself to us and invites us to stretch ourselves and surrender as He molds us according to His beautiful design. Surrender more to God and frequently invite Him into your heart in this life. Focus on the promises of Christ and eternal life with God in all His glory. One certainty in life is that we will all die. Life in our mortal bodies is short, but our next life is eternal in our immortal bodies. Crosses that are taken up with God lead to resurrections. Live life today with eyes directed toward heaven in search of your relationship with God in the mess. Embrace the mess in life with Jesus. Open your eyes and heart to the spiritual realities God wants to reveal, and you will find Jesus in the mess.

Made in the USA
Columbia, SC
03 November 2022